How Noah Saved the Animals

Scenes from the Old Testament

By Hildegard Kretschmer

Prestel

Munich · Berlin · London · New York

How God Created the Earth

In the beginning, God created heaven and earth. He said: "Let there be light." And there was light. God called the light 'day' and called the darkness 'night.' This was the very first day. On the second day, God created a 'heaven' above and, on the third day, he separated water and land to make the earth below. Plants and trees began to grow. On the fourth day, God said: "Let there be lamps in the heavens," and then he created the sun, the moon and the stars. On the fifth day, God made the fish in the oceans and the birds in the sky. Then God said: "Let there be animals on the land, too." And so, on the sixth day, he created all the other animals.

The picture on the opposite page, of the sixth day of creation, was painted by Bertram von Minden more than 600 years ago at a time in history known as the Gothic period. God is blessing the animals he has made so that they will have a good life. Bertram von Minden painted God much larger than the biggest of the animals, but in a way that you can see he is their friend. He is stretching out his right hand to bless them. The way he holds his hand to do this can often be seen in other paintings, too.

Can you recognise all the animals?

On the left of the main picture you can see the animals that live on land. On the right are the animals that live in water and the birds are above them. The birds seem to be sitting in the air and the fish are swimming on a golden background instead of in water. Bertram von Minden simply painted one animal above another. This may look a bit flat to us because we expect some things to look near and others far away. However, most of the animals look very real. Bertram von Minden must have looked at them very carefully before drawing them. Not all artists did this at that time, in fact many just copied illustrations out of other books.

Is this really a picture of God?

Here, God has been painted to look like Jesus with dark hair, a short beard and a cross within a halo. For a long time, artists did not paint pictures of God because in the Ten Commandments it says that this is not allowed – and in any case, no-one knows what God looks like. That is his secret. This is why artists used to draw Jesus to represent God. As Jesus was the Son of God, he was not only God but also a human being, and painting human beings was no problem. When Bertram von Minden was alive, however, most painters were already daring to paint God himself, mostly as an old man with white hair and a white beard.

Why is the background golden?

There is no countryside in this picture. The entire background sparkles with precious gold. This shows that something very special and holy is happening.

Bertram von Minden,
The Creation of the Animals

Bertram von Minden (around 1340–1414/15) lived in Hamburg in the north of Germany. He painted many large pictures for church altars and he was the most important painter of the times in that area. Many other painters copied him. When they painted people and animals they used the same brilliant colours and a very clear, lively style that was very unusual in those days. They also started to make animals look less flat and more like living creatures, paying greater attention to realistic detail.

How God Created Mankind

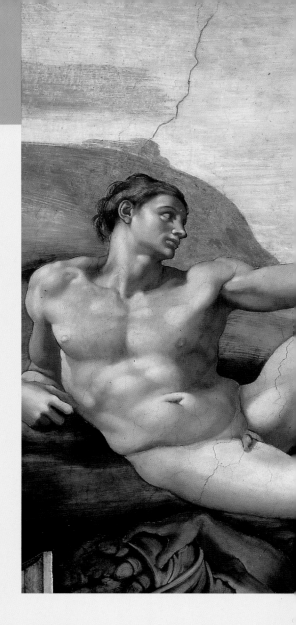

At the end of the seventh day, God created the very first living person. He said: "I will create a man in my own image. He shall be like me. He shall rule the earth." And so God created Adam, the first man. He moulded the dust of the earth to form him and breathed life into him. And then God said: "It is not good to be alone," and so he created a companion called Eve. Then God blessed them and saw that his work was well done. And on the seventh day, he rested.

Michelangelo became a famous artist during his lifetime, about five hundred years ago. When Pope Julius II asked him to paint the ceiling of the chapel in his palace in Rome, Michelangelo wasn't very keen on the idea at first. It was such a large area to paint, and he wasn't actually a painter – he was a sculptor and architect. However, he then went on to paint the story of the creation of the earth, up as far as the story of Noah's ark. He did this in such an outstanding way that this painting became one of the most famous of all times.

A split second!

God's finger stretches across the blue heavens towards Adam's hand. It is as if an electric spark is just about to jump across. This is the moment when Adam really comes to life and God's spirit enters into him. The first person on earth has been created.

How did Michelangelo see the Creation of Mankind?

Michelangelo does not portray God making a man out of clay. In his painting, Adam is already formed. He is lying on the ground, supporting himself on his elbow. God has come down from heaven. He has grey hair and a grey beard. He has a magnificent and powerful presence. God stretches his right hand towards Adam who has raised his hand, but is still weak. Adam looks up to God and God looks down at Adam.

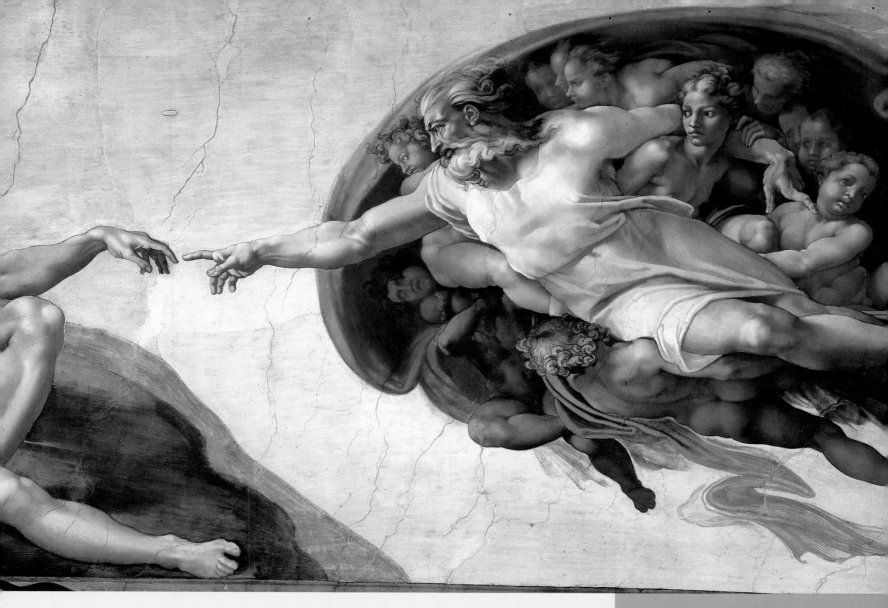

Michelangelo Buonarroti, *The Creation of Man*

Michelangelo painted Adam as a beautiful and already perfectly formed man. His whole body is turned towards God in a way he could almost be a reflection of God himself.
Through this, the artist reminds us of the words of the Bible which say that God created man in his own image.

The name 'Adam' is taken from the Hebrew language in which the Old Testament was originally written. It means 'person made out of red earth'.

Michelangelo Buonarroti (1475–1564) lived and worked in Italy, in Florence and Rome, primarily as a sculptor and an architect. The marble statue of David is one of his most famous works. His best-known paintings are on the ceiling of the Sistine Chapel in the Vatican and depict the Last Judgement. Michelangelo liked painting bold shapes and dramatic poses. But he wasn't just a painter, sculptor and architect; he was also a poet and engineer as well.

How Evil Entered Paradise

Adam and Eve lived in paradise, in the Garden of Eden. God made the most wonderful fruit grow there. Adam and Eve were to look after the garden and cultivate it. But they were not allowed to eat the fruit of the Tree of the Knowledge of Good and Evil. God said to them: "I do not want you to learn of the existence of evil. You must not eat the fruit of this tree, otherwise you will become mortal and will one day die." But then the snake, representing evil, came to tempt them, saying: "If you eat the forbidden fruit, you will become like God and know all things." They liked the idea of this and Eve plucked an apple from the tree. She ate it and gave some to Adam. Afterwards they were ashamed. Now they were afraid of God and tried to hide. When God came, he asked Adam what had happened, but Adam blamed Eve, and Eve blamed the snake. Then God cursed the snake and drove Adam and Eve out of paradise. The first two children born to Adam and Eve were called Cain and Abel. Cain became a farmer and Abel was a shepherd. One day both brothers made a sacrifice to God. The smoke from Abel's sacrifice rose straight to heaven and God was pleased. But God did not like Cain's sacrifice. This made Cain very angry and he hit his brother so hard that he died. This was the first murder of all time. God saw what had happened and condemned Cain to wander around the earth in foreign lands. Cain was afraid that he would be killed, but God put a protective mark on him so that nobody could kill him.

The Tree of Knowledge is to the right of the painting with a branch stretching over Adam and Eve's heads. The fruit of the tree looks very tempting, but a snake is winding up the trunk. The snake has already persuaded Eve to pick an apple. Eve gives it to Adam, but he is unsure. Two animals are watching – a stag can be seen on the left and a lion on the right.

The picture does not tell us what happened next. But perhaps the look in the lion's eyes is an indication that paradise is about to end.

What do you think paradise looks like?

Most people think that paradise is a place where everyone is happy and where nobody suffers. The Bible was originally written in Hebrew, and in Hebrew, the 'Garden of Eden' means 'Garden of Joy'. Traditional stories about a place where people were good and happy are told in many countries world-wide.

Why an apple?

Although the Bible does not actually say what sort of fruit grew on the Tree of Knowledge, most artists over the years have chosen to paint an apple. This is because the Latin word for 'apple' (malum) is the same as the Latin word for 'bad'.

Lucas Cranach the Elder,
Adam and Eve

This picture was
painted nearly five
hundred years ago by
Lucas Cranach the
Elder (1472–1553).
He lived at the Court
of Wittenberg in Sax-
ony, in the east of
Germany, and was
a friend of Martin
Luther. Cranach had
a large art studio and
lots of assistants, but
he also had an inn,
a chemist's shop and
his own printing
business.

The Great Flood

It was not long before there were many people living on the earth. But they were always fighting and arguing. God regretted having made man at all and wanted to destroy everyone. And so he said to Noah, the only good man left: "I am going to wipe all living creatures off the face of the earth, but I will save you. Build a big ship. And when it is finished, climb aboard with your family into this ark, together with one pair of every animal. And take enough food with you for everybody, because I am going to make it rain for forty days and forty nights." And when Noah had finished building the ark, he called his family together and rounded up the animals. Then God sent the flood. It began to rain. The water rose higher and higher and all the other people and animals drowned. Only Noah, his family and the animals on board survived. And when the rain stopped, Noah sent out a raven, and then two doves. The second dove returned holding an olive leaf in its beak and so Noah knew that there must be dry land nearby. It was not long before everyone was able to leave the ark safely. Noah made a sacrifice to God. And then God made an agreement with Noah saying: "I will never again put a curse on the earth. The rainbow which I will put into the sky will be a sign that I will keep this promise to all living creatures."

What a lot of animals! Deer, lions, camels and leopards, wild boars and turkeys, monkeys, birds and tortoises – all the animals have come! I wonder if there will be enough room for everyone in the ark that has been painted right at the back of the picture. In any case, Noah seems to think there is. He is leading them all that way –some animals are in a hurry to get there and others are playing around. The horse is looking the other way, towards us, or perhaps it is just just looking out for its mate.

The painter shows us that the ark will be a place of refuge by letting a bright light shine on it from above. The church, which appears exactly above Noah in the background on the right is also an indication that God is on Noah's side.

In the middle of the picture, Jan Breughel has painted a few people on their way to market. They are having a short rest and are watching Noah and the animals with interest. But they don't seem too surprised. They probably have no idea yet that the flood is on its way.

Stories about a great flood that happened long ago are told all over the world. Many thousands and thousands of years ago, there must have been an enormous flood which covered large parts of the earth.

Jan Breughel the Elder, *The Entry of the Animals into Noah's Ark*

Have you ever seen a picture of a dove holding an olive branch in its beak? This is used all over the world as a symbol of peace. It comes from the story of Noah's Ark.

Jan Breughel the Elder (1568–1625) also painted the picture of Jonah and the whale at the end of this book. Jan Breughel loved painting animals in bright colours. He was court painter to Archduke Albert and Archduchess Isabella, and studying the exotic animals in their zoo enabled him to paint them so vividly. He was also known as 'Flower Breughel' because he painted so many pictures of flowers.

The Story of Abraham

Some years later, in the fertile land of Ur, lived a man called Abraham. God ordered him to leave and go to a different country. Abraham obeyed and travelled to the land of Canaan, taking his wife Sarah and all his cattle with him. And God said to Abraham: "This is the land that I want to give to you and your descendants. I will make a pact with you and you will become the father of many tribes." A son was born to Abraham and Sarah, who were already quite old and who had had no children. They were overjoyed and called him Isaac. When Isaac was a bit older, God decided to test Abraham's faith and said: "Take the son that you love and sacrifice him on the top of the mountain." Abraham was dreadfully shocked, but he wanted to obey God so he set off with his son. Isaac asked his father: "Where is the lamb for the sacrifice." Abraham answered: "God will provide his own sacrifice." At the top of the mountain, Abraham built an altar. Then he took out a knife to kill his son. But at that moment an angel appeared and said: "Abraham! Abraham! Don't harm Isaac! You have obeyed God and were prepared to sacrifice your only son. You will be rewarded and blessed." Abraham suddenly saw a ram nearby, caught in a bush by its horns, and he sacrificed the ram instead. Then he returned home with his son.

This is such a dreadful story that we can hardly bear it, but it does have a happy end. It also became a popular theme for artists. Here Isaac, who is almost naked, has been tied up and is lying on the ground. Abraham, his face pale with horror, is pressing Isaac's head down onto the wooden block. Abraham was prepared to do God's will, but then an angel appears and holds Abraham back and the knife falls out of his hand.

The land of Ur where Abraham lived is in the country presently known as Iraq. Canaan lies about where Israel is today. Abraham and his family were nomads. They lived in tents and moved from one pasture to another. In those days, human sacrifices were still made. Abraham's story shows that the God we know from the Bible does not want these terrible sacrifices, but he does want complete obedience. Because Abraham obeyed, God made him the father of his chosen people.

What is the angel pointing at?

The angel is pointing at the heavens, at the light, and he asks Abraham to stop in the name of God. Abraham has not yet understood that the test is over and that his son will be saved. But to the left we can already see the ram that will take Isaac's place.

The painter Rembrandt and his students painted this picture about 370 years ago. Rembrandt captured the most intense moment in the story. The knife is still poised, aimed at Isaac's throat. A bright light falls on all the important things – Isaac's pale skin, Abraham's grief-stricken face and the angel's hands. And everything seems so dreadfully real and near!

Rembrandt Harmensz. van Rijn (1606–69) was the son of a Dutch miller. Today he is one of the most famous painters in the whole world. He became very rich, as his paintings were worth a lot of money, but later he had great financial problems because his pictures went out of fashion. Unlike many other painters, Rembrandt did not make people more beautiful or wonderful than they really were. He was known especially for his use of contrast – how he painted areas of darkness next to areas of light.

Rembrandt and pupils,
The Sacrifice of Isaac

The Story of Jacob

Isaac married Rebecca who later gave birth to twins. When they were older, Esau, who was the eldest, worked in the fields and went out hunting with his father. Jacob used to stay at home with his mother. He was her favourite child. One day, Esau came back from the hunt completely exhausted. Jacob was cooking lentil soup and Esau wanted to eat some but Jacob, who had always wished he were the first-born son, refused to let Esau eat unless he gave up his birthright. Esau was so desperately hungry that – foolishly – he agreed. Some time later, when Isaac lay on his deathbed, he called his first-born son to give him his blessing. With the help of his mother, Jacob managed to deceive his blind old father into thinking he was Esau and received the special blessing reserved for the first-born son which said: "May God give you dew from heaven and rich soil in your fields. All nations shall serve you. You shall be lord over your brothers and they shall bow down before you." When Esau came and asked for the special blessing, his father could not repeat it because he had already blessed Jacob. Esau swore revenge and Jacob had to leave. Despite this trickery, however, God protected Jacob. Jacob worked for his uncle and became very rich. He married and had twelve sons. And when Jacob wanted to return home, he sent a herd of his finest animals ahead as a present for his brother as a way of saying 'sorry'. He himself did not follow right away. That night, God sent an angel to Jacob and they fought for a long time. But Jacob did not give up and called out: "I will not leave you in peace until you have given me your blessing." And then the angel spoke and said: "Your name shall no longer be Jacob. You shall now be called Israel. For you have proved to God how strong you are." And from that time on, all Jacob's sons and descendants were called 'Israelites'. And when Jacob saw Esau the next day, he bowed very low before him and offered him presents. Esau threw his arms around Jacob's neck and so they were reconciled.

Isaac is old and blind. He is sitting in bed with a fur-lined coat around his shoulders and a blanket on his knees. He has taken off his majestic turban. Before he dies, he wants to give a blessing to his first-born son Esau, but actually it is Jacob who kneels before him!

Will Isaac notice that it is Jacob and not Esau?

Jacob is wearing his brother's clothes and has put gloves on because Esau's hands are much hairier than his own. There is a plate of roast meat on the table behind. Rebecca has cooked this in exactly the same way as Esau cooks for his father. Isaac has taken Jacob's hand, and Jacob looks up at him anxiously, wondering if he will manage to deceive him. But he need not worry. Isaac is already saying the traditional blessing for the first-born son.

Is everything going according to plan? The woman in the background is Rebecca, the mother of the twins. She is hovering and watching Isaac's reaction. It looks like her plan is working.

What are the people thinking or feeling?

Although this is a very calm picture with little or no movement, the painter Govaert Flinck has managed to tell us part of the story through the different expressions on people's faces. The blind father is looking inwards rather than towards his outer surroundings. Jacob looks worried. Rebecca looks on confidently, waiting to see what happens. We are drawn into the picture and are witnesses to the scene.

Govaert Flinck, *Isaac blesses Jacob*

The traditional blessing for the first-born son speaks of the 'dew from heaven' and 'rich soil.' Dew and rich soil were very important in Canaan, a land with very little rainfall. Often, dew was the only water. According to the law of that time, the eldest son received most of his father's wealth and possessions, replacing him as head of the family after his death.

Govaert Flinck (1615–60) was born in Cleves in northern Germany, but later he went to Holland, to Amsterdam, where he studied painting under Rembrandt. At the height of his career he was highly regarded for his portraits and he also painted many Biblical scenes. People thought he was even better than Rembrandt, his teacher. In fact, he was thought the best painter in Amsterdam! Today he is not so well known, whereas many more people have heard of Rembrandt.

The Story of Joseph

Jacob had twelve sons. Joseph, who was a dreamer, was his favourite and this made the others very jealous. One day they threw him into a dried up well and sold him later as a slave. They then smeared Joseph's coat with the blood of a young goat and brought it to their father so that he would think that he had been killed by a wild animal. Meanwhile, Joseph had to work as a slave for Potiphar in Egypt. Because he worked so well, Joseph was made an administrator, but Potiphar's wife brought accusations against him and he was put into prison. There, Joseph talked to the other prisoners about their dreams and told them what they meant. When the Pharaoh, the Egyptian King, heard about this, he called Joseph to him and told him about his dream; seven fat cows had been eaten by seven thin cows, and seven fat ears of corn had been swallowed by seven dried up ears of corn. Joseph told the Pharaoh that he would have seven years of plenty followed by seven years during which there would be little to eat. He told the Pharaoh to store all the extra food from the years of plenty in big barns, so that there would be extra food for the years of famine. In the years that followed, it was exactly as Joseph had foretold, so the Pharaoh made him chief administrator of all Egypt. And when the famine came, Joseph was able to provide food. Joseph's brothers travelled to Egypt to buy food, but they did not recognise their brother. Joseph decided to test them. He secretly hid a silver cup in the sack of food carried by Benjamin, the youngest brother. On their way home, the brothers were followed. They were searched and accused of stealing the silver cup, and Benjamin was to be made a slave. But all the other brothers turned round and came back, and Judah offered to become a slave instead of Benjamin. This showed Joseph that they had had a real change of heart, and then he told them who he really was. And in the end he was reunited with his old father Jacob who was brought to live with him in Egypt.

The picture shows five of the brothers showing Joseph's coat to their father. He is an elegant, dignified man. He is sitting in a large hall. There is a richly decorated carpet on the marble floor. Jacob is throwing his arms in the air in horror. He is filled with fear and terror as he stares at the blood on the coat. It belongs to Joseph, his favourite son – who must have been killed, or so he thought!

Why is the small white dog barking so much?

Perhaps he knows that the brothers are not telling the truth. They all look really sad and can see how upset their father is. Although they are playing a trick, perhaps they also feel very ashamed.

Diego Velázquez, *Joseph's Bloodstained Coat is brought to Jacob*

The Spanish artist Diego Velázquez (1599–1660) made the figures in his painting very large. They seem close to us and totally real. The brothers are standing in front of us like actors on a stage and we have the feeling that we are standing there next to them. Perhaps we are supposed to be one of the missing brothers, joining in the action. Is this why Velázquez did not paint all of them? Did he paint the strong light and dark shadows to make us feel even more horrified?

Velázquez is one of the most famous of all Spanish painters. While he was living in his hometown, Seville, he tended to draw scenes of everyday life. But then he went to Madrid to serve the king. He was made a member of court and painted portraits, religious pictures and scenes from ancient tales. These were themes fit for a king. Velázquez was actually more of a courtier than a painter and painting took second place to his court duties.

17

The Story of Moses

Jacob's descendants in Egypt turned into a prosperous nation, but the Pharaoh wanted them to be slaves because he was worried that they would soon outnumber the Egyptians. He was so worried that he ordered all their new-born baby boys to be killed. This is why one Israelite mother decided to put her little son in a basket and left him in the bulrushes on the banks of the river Nile. The daughter of the Pharaoh came and discovered the basket and she decided that he would become her son. She called him Moses. He grew up in the palace like a prince, but his people still bore much suffering. One day, Moses saw an Egyptian overseer treating an Israelite badly. Moses was so angry that he attacked him and killed him. Then he ran away from the palace and lived in the hills as a shepherd. One day when he was herding his sheep up a mountain, Moses saw a burning bush which didn't actually burn up. A voice told him to take off his shoes. Then it said: "I am the God of your father, the God of Abraham, the God of Isaac and the God of Jacob. I can hear the cries of my children, the Israelites. Lead them out of Egypt to a land of milk and honey." Moses returned to Egypt and demanded that the Pharaoh let his people go. The Pharaoh refused, and so God sent ten dreadful plagues to Egypt, including an angel who killed all the first-born sons in Egypt. The Israelites were told to eat unleavened bread – which is quick to make – and paint the blood of a lamb on their doors so that their sons would not be killed by the angel. In the end the Pharaoh agreed to let the Israelites go. Today, Jews celebrate the festival of Passover to remember how they were delivered from Egypt long ago.

What a handsome procession! The daughter of the Pharaoh has arrived, followed by her servants. She is beautiful and proud. And what lovely clothes she has on! The princess seems even more beautiful compared with the old servant woman and ugly dwarf standing at her side.

Is this what Egyptian princesses really looked like?

The painter, Tiepolo, lived in the eighteenth century and probably had no idea what the Egyptians wore. His Egyptian princess is wearing the sort of dress worn by rich women in his hometown of Venice in the sixteenth century. Tiepolo wasn't so much interested in the story itself, but in the effect that it had.

Giovanni Battista Tiepolo,
Finding Moses

But the picture also tells another story:

We can see the servant holding little Moses. She is pointing to a girl. She is called Miriam and is Moses' elder sister, but the Egyptians don't know this. She had hidden herself near the basket to look after Moses. Now Miriam is telling the princess that she knows a woman who could breastfeed Moses. And so Moses finds his way back to his own mother. When he was a bit older, he was taken to live at the palace with the princess.

Giovanni Battista Tiepolo (1696–1770) was the most famous Venetian painter of the eighteenth century. His murals and paintings are created in a very imaginative way with elegant lines and brilliant colours. Many of his figures strike poses as if they are on stage. Tiepolo worked in Würzburg and Madrid as well as in Italy.

The Ten Commandments

Moses is coming down from Mount Sinai clutching the tablets on which God's commandments are written, surrounded by a bright light.

When Moses led the Israelites out of Egypt, the Pharaoh regretted letting all his slaves go, so he followed them with his army. They caught up with the Israelites on the banks of the Sea of Reeds. And God said to Moses: "Hold your stick out across the sea, for I will divide it." The waters parted for the Israelites to cross, but when the Egyptians tried to follow, the waters rolled back and drowned them. Then the Israelites had to cross a large desert. When they reached Mount Sinai, God ordered Moses to climb the mountain. A great storm broke and amid thunder and lightening God gave Moses his commandments written on two stone tablets. But because Moses had been away on the mountain for such a long time, the people became restless and began to make a golden calf as an image of their God. When Moses came down from the mountain he saw them dancing round the calf and was so angry that he flung down the tablets. Then people were sorry for what they had done. God forgave them and gave Moses two new tablets. Then the Israelites started to carry out God's command to build a beautiful tabernacle to house the tablets. After Moses', Joshua became the leader of the nation of Israel and led them to Canaan, the land God had promised them. Canaan was divided into twelve, one part for each of the twelve tribes called after Jacob's twelve sons. They called their leaders judges, but God was their master.

The Ten Commandments

You shall not have any other God but me.
You shall not make or worship any image of me.
You shall not make wrong use of the name of God.
Keep Sundays as a day of rest.
Respect your father and mother.
You shall not kill.
You shall love your own husband or wife, not someone else's.
You shall not steal.
You shall not tell any lies about anyone else.
You shall not long for or take anything or anyone belonging to someone else.

What is this little boy doing?

Moses climbed up and down the mountain three times in all. This picture shows him coming down with the tablets and, this time, everyone is waiting for him. Some are praying and others are lifting up their hands towards him. Some are kneeling down. The little boy seems to be looking on in complete amazement.

Why was this picture painted?

This painting was commissioned for the Town Hall of Amsterdam. When the hall was built, the people of Amsterdam wanted to hang pictures in it that showed its citizens how to live together in harmony. This picture of Moses and the tablets was painted for the Court of Justice as a reminder of how important it is to obey God's laws.

What do the Ten Commandments mean?

At that time, the people in Israel's neighbouring countries used to worship statues and pictures of lots of different gods. But Israel only had one God and nobody was allowed to make an image of him. God's laws showed the Israelites how to behave so that they could live together in peace.

Ferdinand Bol (1616–80) was a painter and engraver who lived in Amsterdam. He worked for Rembrandt before he decided to start out on his own. Sometimes the styles of the two painters are so similar that it is difficult to tell them apart. Bol was often asked to paint portraits or murals for the walls of public buildings. When his wife died, he married another lady who was so rich that he didn't need to earn money through painting any more.

Ferdinand Bol,
Moses holding the Stone Tablets

David and Goliath

Later on, the Israelites forgot God and their agreement with him. They wanted to have a king like the other nations. God was not happy about this, but he allowed his prophet Samuel to anoint a young man named Saul as king. Saul became a great commander and won many battles against Israel's enemies. The prophet also anointed a young shepherd from Bethlehem by the name of David. He was to become the next king. In those days, the Israelites were fighting against the Philistines led by their commander, the giant, Goliath. Goliath sneered at the Israelites and announced that he wanted to fight their strongest man. Everyone was afraid. Only David was prepared to take up the fight against him. His only weapons were his shepherd's crook and a sling. Goliath laughed at the young shepherd, but David got out his sling. He aimed a stone at Goliath and it struck his forehead with such force that he fell. Then David took Goliath's sword and killed him. When they saw this, the Philistines fled and the Israelites rejoiced. David married Michal, the daughter of Saul, and became the second King of Israel after Saul's death. For the most part he was a good ruler of Israel. He was also a great poet and played the harp. Many of the psalms in the Bible were written by him.

David is kneeling beside the giant. Goliath is still alive. His helmet has fallen off and his armour is glinting in the light. The blood on his forehead is glowing red. David is about to kill Goliath with his own sword. In the distance the soldiers of the Philistines can be seen fleeing. The painter Guido Reni portrays the story very simply but vividly, contrasting small, unarmed David with the enormous, armour-covered Goliath. He also contrasts light with shade and brighter colours with darker tones to great effect. However, Reni did not just want to capture this particular moment. He wanted to present David as the great hero of the Israelites, a symbol of how the weaker can win against the strong. And so David stands proud and upright, dressed in red. He almost looks like a statue. Today, David is still seen as a symbol of the fight for justice, even if the outlook seems hopeless.

Guido Reni,
David Slaying Goliath

Was David afraid?

In the picture he looks quite calm and confident. He is wearing a red tunic even though only kings were allowed to wear red. He is certain to win the fight as Goliath has been badly wounded. Reni has painted him in dark colours, nearly the same colours as the ground he is lying on.

Guido Reni (1575–1642) was an Italian painter during the Baroque period. He worked in Rome and Bologna. In his early painting days, he was influenced by the painter Caravaggio's methods of contrasting light and dark colours, as this painting shows. Later he tended to use lighter colours. Although his name is not familiar to most people today, Reni became well-known during his lifetime and well into the late 19th century as a result of his memorable religious paintings in which the main figures often turned their eyes towards heaven.

The Wisdom of Solomon

When David died, his son Solomon became king in his place. God appeared to Solomon in a dream and said that he would grant Solomon a wish. Solomon, who was still very young, wished that he might become a wise and just king. God was pleased that Solomon had not asked for riches or a long life, so he gave him not only wisdom but riches and a long life too. One day two women came to King Solomon. They lived in the same house and had given birth to baby boys at the same time. But one of the women's babies had died and the mother secretly exchanged the dead child for the living one. The second woman knew that the dead child was not hers and so the two woman fought over the child that was still alive. King Solomon called for a sword. "You shall both have half a child each!" he said. One of the women was deeply shocked and cried "No! Don't kill the child! I would rather my neighbour had it." When he heard this, Solomon knew that the woman was the child's real mother and gave her back the child. Under Solomon's reign there was peace and justice throughout the land. Solomon built a huge temple in God's honour in Jerusalem. Following Solomon's death, Israel became divided into two, the north and the south, and the people forgot God.

Here we can see the young king Solomon sitting in judgement on his throne. He is about to make a decision. But how can he tell which woman is the real mother? He knows how best to find out and calls for the child to be cut into two. A soldier is already holding it by its foot. Everyone is in a state of shock.

The artist shows Solomon weighing up the situation carefully knowing that he will reach a fair judgement. In the same way the artist composes his painting in a very balanced way. Solomon is sitting in the middle, flanked by symmetrical columns and architecture. The figures in the painting have strong outlines and the colours are very clear. This all points to a fair decision.

Who is the real mother?

The mother on the right is wearing red and green. She is holding
the dead child carelessly under her arm. Her face is grey and angry.
She is pointing at the other woman accusingly and is arguing with
her. The other mother kneels in shock in front of the child that is to
be sliced into two. She stretches out her arms to plea with the king.
Her clothes are painted in a clear blue, white and yellow. She must
be the real mother! The gestures of the figures are very dramatic
and rather exaggerated, but they show us quite clearly what people
are feeling or thinking.

Nicolas Poussin (1594–1665) was a French-
man, but he lived most of his life in Rome.
There he painted scenes from ancient legends,
religious themes and landscapes. Poussin was
very well educated. His painting had a very
rigid and formal style and he greatly admired
ancient classical art. His solemn style made
him the most famous French painter of the
Baroque period.

Judith and Holofernes

In the years which followed, a number of prophets tried to make Israel turn to God, but the Israelites cursed and persecuted them. Then foreign armies tried to conquer Israel's cities. Holofernes, the commander of the Assyrian army, had surrounded the city of Betulia. The wells were also under his control and so the citizens had nothing to drink. Then they turned to God for help. Just as the city was about to surrender, a good widow called Judith set about saving the city. She put on magnificent clothes and went to Holofernes' army camp with her servant. She promised to show the Assyrians the way into Betulia if she was allowed to go to Holofernes' tent. Judith was very beautiful. Holofernes liked her and believed what she said. After three days, he held a banquet for her and wanted her to spend the night with him. But he drank so much that he fell into a deep sleep. When his servant had gone to bed, Judith took Holofernes' sword and cut off his head. She put it in a sack, left the camp and went back to Betulia. Holofernes' head was hung from the city walls. The Assyrians were so terrified that they fled, and Betulia was free again. Not long afterwards, Jerusalem and Solomon's temple were destroyed by Nebuchadnezzar. Many people were taken to Babylon and forced to work as slaves. The king made some of them his advisors and one of these was Daniel who was able to interpret the dreams of the king.

It is nighttime and everything is in darkness. The curtain in front of Holofernes' tent has been pulled back and we are witness to a horrible scene. Judith has just cut off Holofernes' head and is about to put it into the sack held by her maid.

A dreadful crime

A bright light is falling on Judith. She looks young, beautiful and is very well dressed – a lovely sight! Can Judith be seen as a heroine despite what she has just done? How do you think she feels?

Paolo Veronese (1528–88) was one of the most important painters in Venice in the middle of the 16th century alongside Titian and Tinoretto. He painted scenes from many biblical stories, pictures from ancient myths and legends, and frescoes for churches, palaces, and villas. Veronese had a strong influence on many artists in the 18th century, just like Tiepolo.

Just like David, Judith has always been seen as a heroine who rescued her people. As a result of her bravery she spared her town from a terrible fate. But despite this, it was still murder. The artist Paolo Veronese senses both the good and the bad sides to this story in his painting of Judith and does not portray her as the triumphant saviour as many other artists did.

Paolo Veronese, *Judith with the Head of Holofernes*

The Mysterious Message Written in Fire

One day, when King Belshazzar, the son of Nebuchadnezzar, had drunk too much at a banquet, he ordered the gold and silver goblets that his father had stolen from the temple of Jerusalem to be brought out. Then he and his friends drank to the gods they worshipped in their own country. Suddenly a hand appeared and wrote words in fire on the wall. The king was very afraid. He called for his fortune-teller and astrologer, but they couldn't read the writing. Then he remembered Daniel. Daniel told the king that he had sinned against God because he had used the temple vessels to drink to their own self-made gods. Then Daniel read the writing. It said 'Mene mene tekel u-parsin', which means 'counted – weighed – divided'. The days of the king were counted. God would put an end to his reign. Belshazzar had been weighed up by God and found lacking. His kingdom would be split and would fall to the Medians and Persians. That night the king was murdered. The new Persian king appointed Daniel as his chief minister. The others became jealous of Daniel and convinced the Persian king that he alone should be worshipped, but Daniel prayed only to God. The king wanted to protect Daniel, but Daniel was breaking his law and had to be thrown to the lions. But the lions did not touch him. When the king saw that God was protecting Daniel he threw the jealous officials to the lions instead and proclaimed that from now on, Daniel's God should be the only God.

What is happening here?

King Belshazzar has just jumped up with shock and is filled with panic and fear. He is looking at the strange hand writing fiery letters on the wall. He has just knocked over one of the holy vessels from the temple of Jerusalem, spilling wine on the table. The woman on the right has knocked her wine over too. What will happen next? The party atmosphere has been shattered. Nobody understands the writing on the wall, but they all know that something terrible is about to happen. The musicians in the background are the only ones who haven't noticed anything yet.

What does the writing mean?

The painter, Rembrandt, manages to worry us, too. Can you read this writing? It is written in Hebrew but the words are written from top to bottom, and not from right to left as is usual in Hebrew. Daniel is the only person who can interpret the writing, but he is not in the picture. The painter captures the most exciting moment in the story and then leaves us in suspense.

Rembrandt, *The Feast of King Belshazzar*

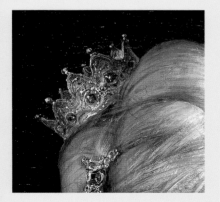

Why was this picture painted?

In the 17th century when this picture was painted, rich people in Holland liked to surround themselves with paintings which warned against extreme behaviour or announced some sort of judgement. This painting with its banqueting table probably hung in a dining room. At that time, the rooms were not so bright as nowadays because they were only lit by candlelight, and so the painting must have looked almost real!

See page 13 for more information on Rembrandt Harmensz. van Rijn.

29

Jonah and the Whale

Some time later, the Jews were allowed to return home from their exile in Babylon. The story of the prophet Jonah comes from this period. God told Jonah to go to Nineveh and warn the people that if they did not mend their ways and worship the true God, they would have great misfortune. But Jonah did not want to go because Nineveh was home to the Assyrians who were enemies of Israel. Instead, he boarded a ship in the opposite direction. God sent such a terrible storm that everyone was afraid. When Jonah realised that he was the reason for the storm, he told the sailors to throw him overboard. The storm stopped and God sent a whale which swallowed Jonah whole! Jonah prayed for three days inside the stomach of the whale, promising God that he would go to Nineveh. Then the whale spat him out on dry land and Jonah set off for Nineveh. He ordered the people to change their ways and worship God and they repented. But Jonah was not happy. He went away and made a shelter of branches to protect himself from the heat. God made a plant grow over it to give Jonah shade. But the following day, the plant died and Jonah was very angry. And God said, "Are you upset about the plant you did not sow yourself? And do you expect me not to pity the poor people of Nineveh?" Then Jonah understood that God cared for all people of all nations. Later, when the Greeks and Romans brought great suffering to Israel, its people continued to believe that God would one day send a saviour to rescue them.

The early Christians were very familiar with the story of Jonah. For them, Jonah's escape from the stormy sea and his three days in the whale's stomach were a parallel to Christ's resurrection from the dead after three days.

Jan Brueghel the Elder (1568–1625) was the son of the famous painter Pieter Brueghel. Jan also painted the picture of the flood. He was an official court painter in southern Holland. Because he painted many pictures of flowers, he is also known as 'Flower Brueghel.'

Clouds are piling up and threatening to burst over the stormy sea. Everything is dark. The only lighter area in the painting falls on a huge whale with its mouth wide open. A frightened old man can be seen climbing out. It is Jonah.

Jan Breughel the Elder,
Jonah and the Whale